Moonli

A Poetry Collection

TERAZA FAULKNER

DEDICATION

This book is dedicated to my husband, parents, sisters,
nieces/nephew, friends (particularly Sandra & Roger) and
my support network/followers on social media.

A special thankyou to Karen Richards of
@words_of_untouched_galaxies
for her unwavering support.

Without the love of and encouragement from
those around me, I may never have had the
courage to share my poetry with the world.

I thank you all, wholeheartedly.

These words are for you

CONTENTS

CHAPTER ONE

All This Love

I rest my head
against the night,
the crescent moon
keeps my dreams alive

waiting for love to come to light

I hold the night close.

I've sprinkled grains
of stardust in the wind,
hoping it may all come back to me,
and the sense of something more
follows its lead

because, sometimes,
love is in the air, just waiting
for a little nudge from somewhere,

just longing to land
in the palm of someone's hand

just longing to land, right here.

stars are like
sparkling
reminders that
big things need not
be such in size

and that
constellations can
fit within the
depth of hearts
and width of eyes

every look can be
that falling star

every touch can be
that dream coming true

when you believe in love.

imagine a love
so strong,

the intensity of your heart
drumming to its
very own song,

beckoning the walls
of your chest
to cave in,

what a beautiful disaster

unravelling.

they say we find love
in the most unexpected places
and I am searching this land
looking down at cracked earth
seeing possibilities
that may lie
between these lines and I

because, if flowers can blossom
in anomalous places

then perhaps, love can too.

the stars press against our hearts,
the place where all this magic starts,
listening to our chests, rise and fall

we fold into our sleep
whilst our dreams come to life

and we wait for *that* star to fall

we imagine opening our eyes

to *the one*

that holds it all.

in dreams, we enter a world
that is entirely ours
sprinkled in stardust –
where the night sky
becomes our wonderlust

and within the folds
of our sheets,
our hearts loudly beat

calling out to those fallen stars,
hoping they hear us,
hoping they sugar our dreams

with their cosmic realm.

I've tugged at the night sky
longing for something
to fall,
like baiting fish
with a line,
hoping I'd catch
a star of some kind

but one must remember,
love cannot be pulled in
any direction
it must gracefully move
until it finds its right home,

that place of connection.

I carry my heart,
as though I am
holding a star.

it dangles with hope,
that little things still
shine from afar.

as small as it is,
pressed against the
vast night sky,

perhaps a galaxy is seen
when there is

love

in those eyes.

it may be written in the stars
but the heart is the beat
behind every word.

drumming to the sound of love
they transcribe
our symphony from above

like musical notes

cascading into the night.

I am that leaf
facing the wind,
tumbling aimlessly
through the air

longing for loving hands,
to save me from
somewhere

for the ground
is rife with burrows
and darkness, to which I run

I need a security net
to catch me,

and face me towards the sun.

an ocean
will always
remind me of love.

waves cascade
through those peaks and troughs.

but they always greet the shore
with a peaceful embrace.

just like a lover's kiss,

after a storm.

his smile
is my crescent moon,
caressing every wound.

now these worn-out scars
have become like stars,
rewriting my song
from the start.

those ambulating notes
that had once
shackled my throat,
now fade against a tune

I can finally sing to.

dreams are not
always big.

they do not have
to be laced
in stardust and magic.

they can be as simple
as blades of grass
caressing your toes
and the relief that abounds
when your feet finally hit
the ground.

because sometimes,
love makes you rise to places

you wish only to fall from.

have you ever walked
on sand and felt the
euphoria of golden hues
kissing your toes and
sinking within their curves,
as if grains of the earth
are transforming
to the very shape
of you?

have you ever felt
a love quite as soft as that,
where every touch
presses gently
against your bones,
softly etching love
to your most hardened parts?

well, if you believe
in love, then you
can believe in this –

the feathering
strokes of softness
can paint all kinds of things

even love stories,
onto the most brittle bones

just like the sand, between your toes.

I have finally found
the most delicate kind.

his soft wings
are gently pressed against mine.

the sky may storm.
the wind may scorn.

but with tender love

such strength

is born.

he whispers my name
and a wind cascades,
like a sand storm
against my spine.

tickling my skin
and engraining his love,

onto my bones

my heart

my *everything.*

cradled
in my blanket of doom
you found me here
like the night seeks the moon

and illuminated the dark
within my folds of gloom.

from front to back,
we form our own

crescent shaped spoon.

when I say 'I love you',
I am saying that –

my every inhale is soaking you in,
cradling you within my cavities

and my every exhale, is just a pause,
a sweet prelude to more

of you.

I do not have to always see,
to realize the beauty before me.

sometimes it's just a touch,

sometimes it's just a voice,

like yours.

I feel love
bounce off my chest,
like sunbeams
that attempt to awaken
the dead.

bringing light to a
cage of dark,
and tunnelling warmth
to where despair
once filled my heart.

I've pressed myself
against these petals of you,
willing your color
to rub off on me.

hoping I'm wild enough,
to grow love
from these
shades of you,
that always fill
my room and
bring light to my dark,

just like the moon.

he has woven
strands of love
around my cuts
to halt their bleeding.

he has tied the knot, tight.
he is showing me these scars,

need not cry.

you are my every sunrise
that I long to greet
and my every sunset
I wished would never leave.

you are both

a beginning and ending
rolled into one.

a cycle I could never tire of.

there was a time I needed
a galaxy of stars
just to catch a glimpse
of hope in my eyes.

but now I have your hand,
and we walk this land,
stepping over cracked earth,
and building bridges on top of
open turf.

now, I no longer need the stars,
the tables have turned
and they now need us.

there is a story waiting to
be written in stardust.

it's called love,

and it is all about us.

before that moment
there was barely a shimmer,
my heartbeat was weak,
these lungs inhaled more pain
than they released.

but a look
was all it took.

almond-shaped stardust
met with mine.
those eyes became
my kryptonite,
those eyes became

my fire.

when I look into your eyes,
these emotions become
hard to describe,

as though my lips
only quiver against
the intensity of such lines.

but if my soul could speak,
it would be like magic.

incising every letter
in a shimmer, so bold

that when the words fall
so too, would those

flakes of gold.

I feel his beating heart
even distances apart

its rhythm in sync with my own.

that heart of his
is intertwined with mine
and a love like this
makes our beats combine

a love like ours always strums
two beats as one.

my heart fits in the palm
of his tender hands.
no longer do I immerse or hide.

for to be held with love

I can rise above.

for to be held with love

I am born.

now, even the moon
reminds me of you,
for she makes
the dark fade
even when the sun
has fallen through.

she makes everything shine,

just like you do.

the essence of you and I,
clears every cloudy sky.

bypassing the grey,
chauffeuring me back

to the light of day.

I am those pearls
being held together,

and you are that
cord that intertwines
my all.

your love is
my string,
my everything.

your love is
what makes me shine.

and without your thread,
I'm falling.

without your love,
my pearls

scatter in the wind.

your eyes are those
gleaming roads
that lead to
sunny pastures.

where the wind
whispers our names,
like music beating
against blades of grass.

a symphony

that defines us.

you are the sunshine
that filters through
the tips of these trees,
showing me –

there is always light to find.

there is always love seeping through

this forest of mine.

we lay pressed
against the grass,
with the glory
of the night sky
before us.

you get lost
in the beauty above,
and I get lost

in your stardust.

I can see the sun
in your eyes,
whether it is day
or night.

I can see a million
galaxies
staring at me.

for there is something
about your love
that takes me
to the skies above.

opens to the sun
folds into the night
it's all in the way

your eyes

meet with mine.

dip me in every shade
of your soul
and may there be
no storm, strong enough
to wash that kind of depth away
no storm, wild enough

to tear us apart.

there is

a place I feel loved,
without being told.

a place I feel wrapped,
without being held.

its language is as
silent as the night.

but its energy
surpasses every light.

here, within this space-

is *that* place,

I call *us*.

you are all mine,

like a flower
planted just for me.

your petals bloom
when I cannot find
the color inside of me.

your stem, the only thing
that keeps me standing
when my feet miss the ground.

your roots, the stampede
for life's weeds to dissipate.

you are so much more than
just the beauty of your blooms.

let me tell you,

your flower, is my everything.

if only you could see me
holding out my heart,
longing for you to impart
its weight in love.

if only there was a measure that
could quantify such,
something stronger than just
words or my touch.

staggering on this tight rope of 'love',
I sway to the left and from above,
there is nothing but blooms,
no doom or gloom in sight.

moving along, I sway to the right,
and find amongst even the darkest
of nights, blooms still sprouting to life
without the need for light.

is this the rope that differentiates?

is this the line that I continually break?

one of these days I will figure it out.

perhaps my garden of love

is where all those miracles sprout.

TERAZA FAULKNER

CHAPTER TWO

All This Loss & Pain

winter has woven
its way around me,
and now I bear tears
of stone-cold disbelief.

how did love make
such a season of me?

how did love escape
what was born from

sunbeams?

I fold myself
into the creases you left,
like a flower
closing into a bud.

desperately
wanting to recreate
the shape of our love.

but to bloom again,
I need more
than just remnants
of love.

I need a heart.

I need a touch.

I need you.

if I gather all of our feathers,
can I put us back together?

or did those storms behind our wings,
shatter every little thing?

what happened to our fire?
did those winds steal our desire?

tell me, how can we return to the sky?

the meadow still bears our footsteps
as though the wild has tattooed
our love on the ground

and it is there that I still feel,

my feet touch yours.

pressed to my palm,
I hold this
lavender sprig tight,
hoping I can preserve
the only piece of devotion
left between us.

our field now barren,
but if this sprig could speak,
it would call out
to our emptiness
and pray for an echo back,

anything to suggest
there is still some love left.

still a chance that

our field can grow back from this sprig.

it's true.
spring was always
just around the corner.

but,

the birds were never meant to sing.
the flowers were never meant to bloom.

with you.

how do I blow out that candle
that incessantly burns
just for you?

these wisps of yesterday,
give me something to hold onto.

how do I live with an exhale,
that makes nothingness, come true?

how do I blow out forever,
when my forever was always you?

his memory,

an endless echo,
reverberating against
my every bone,
shaking all
the broken bits,
filling those voids
that his desertion left.

as though, within me
he continues to roam,

and my ruins have become his home.

I stare into your eyes
and see dusk
fold behind their lines,

waiting for your
glow, your horizon
to show.

if only I knew how
to meet you at
that line,

at that point, it all
fades and omits
the shine.

then maybe you
would have
been less of
what I could barely see,

and more like a
horizon that melted

into me.

pain does not always roar

even butterflies
carry wounds
disguised by colorful wings
and a graceful silence.

we lost the sea at our feet.
the sand barely even scraped
the surface of our curiosities.

torn between waves too high
and tides too far out
to dip our feet in,

we never gave ourselves the chance
to be swept out by the sea
and tumble within
all of its possibilities.

we never gave ourselves the chance at anything.

salty tears
fall between these lines,
and I've counted too many times
the number of letters
that can look like your name
but also feel like pain.

I wish I had the words to explain
this empty page.

I wish I had the words to explain –

you.

like morning fog blankets
the beauty of a new day,
I still wake to your memory,
like it was yesterday.

the hours pass
and sunlight fills the sky,
but these eyes
still hold the weight

of that goodbye.

this ticket came
etched in stardust.

this pass was
laced with dreams
for us.

if only I had known
how quickly
magic blew away.

if only I had known
how easily

our stars would fade.

I hold the rain
against these
tears.

knowing
I am not alone
helps me reach
that closure line.

the sky is so far away,
but she knows my pain
more than you do.

she cries with me
underneath
these salty sheets.

now all that is left of me,
all that is left of you,

are these tears.

I held on

believing you were my light.

when in essence, this chest
you rested your head against,
was my sole source of fire.

it lit from within
and shone light onto
everything.

like a heart that holds the moon to its chest.

oblivious to the darkness.

this piercing silence
cuts through the air,
and here I am
still dipped in
this ink of despair.

it is amazing
how pain always seems
to find its
voice, in some way.

even if it is
just pen to page,

it's a channel, I can trust.
it's a chapter, I must write

before I can

shut.

if she could crawl
inside her
tear-stained pillow,
she would.

because every drop
spoke more of him
than of her.

and sometimes, you just long
to hear their voice once more.

to sink into their every word,

like never before.

I snuggle with this pain
as though it is here to stay,

kissing it goodnight,
never wishing it away.

I find, if I hold it tight,
it feels just like you,

and if it gets me through the night,
then that's the price
I'm prepared to pay

just to hold you in some way.

this empty void
becomes hard to explain,
when nothingness
feels more like
a mass of pain.

I had never felt such weight
in any goodbye
than that which made 'us'
become 'you and I'.

I guess I never really let go
of our final kiss,
and this must be
the weight of me
still pressed against

your lips.

you were the bark,
I, the tree.
and you slowly
wrapped your way
around me.

the tighter you wound,
the closer you got
to a heart,
a little less lonely.

but seasons change,
and so does love
and you fell from me
like a dying dove.

piece by piece,
you broke away,
and
piece by piece

I died.

if only

these crests of despair
actually led somewhere

perhaps, to a dusk out there
beyond the pain,
where those comforting hues

form a frame,

I can finally walk through.

now

when I say your name,
it feels like something I borrowed.

like a book I never got to read.

but there are some stories
that are just not meant for me.

some stories that end,
before they even have a chance

to begin.

I've fallen
into this space,
the sea between you and I,
between love and loss,

the line that either
draws us together
or pulls us apart,

like the wind
that breaks the leaf in half,
cutting its cord
right at that vital vein,

tearing one into two
and blowing
each further away.

how quickly
time can turn lines
into gaps and then
distances as vast as this sea
that now separates

you from me.

those fireflies
we had conceived,
have slowly
lost their chemistry.

my cord
has been
cut from yours.

now destiny cries,
and so do I.

if only these
puddles reflected

that light.

winter was born
between the
cracks you left.

clouds formed within
my idle mind, and
empty spaces
grew all the
things I wished
had died.

my heart, now heavy
but not from carrying
more love.
just holding all the
pain was more than
enough.

I keep you here
between the empty
and the full,

the paradox between
love and pain,

the bridge between
you and I,

and everything.

there is a wound
beneath my skin.

it whispers.
it screams.

some days it bleeds.
some days it weeps.

it's everything and more
of what we ever were,
because a cut this great
is like a lifeline,

that never breaks.

if only those fireflies
could fill this room
and give me hope
of something more
than just four walls
and one heart.

because those stars
seem so far away,

and so do you.

I am more beautiful
with these tears
rolling down my face.

for the truth is
always prettier
than a lie.

I still bleed inside
for the hurt stems deep,
but my face no
longer hides
what my heart had denied,

for so long.

these tears
fall like rain
upon a windowsill.
cascading down my cheeks,
caressing my lips, releasing
that bitter taste of all of this.

but there are heavier emotions
that fall at a far greater rate.
they seep within,
molding to my fragility.

turning these bones, brittle and porous.
these muscles, weak and sore.

I guess my heart is just crying out to be heard

a little more.

my head may be
just above water,
yet my heart longs
to drown.

I guess it's all
of our memories
still floating around.

how very ironic
life can be,
when the very thing
that wanes us
is what keeps us alive.

it is what keeps us

from *drowning*.

I hold these memories
like storing old books away,

folding back the corners of every
painful page.

hoping just enough air
reaches those lines of despair.

hoping just enough air

keeps our hearts beating there.

the rain bellows
outside, as though
it knows it must
work hard enough
to drown both
tears and your voice.

but it cannot
wash away your
heart from mine,
no matter
how hard it tries.

for some things
do not make a noise,
some things
do not cry.

they just bleed on the inside,

like a silent demise.

I weep for
what I cannot have,
yet fail to acknowledge
what I do.

my heart still beats.
the sun beams
reach my feet.
I wake to a new day
full of promise
and opportunities.

yet my eyes are
ladened by the despair
of a world I
cannot see distinctly.

I wish I could wipe my
eyes and they stay clear.
I wish I could look
in the mirror and realize

all that I need

is right here.

my love still exists,
this longing is endless.

like a garden of blooms
that are eternal.

like a heart that holds a flame
these lungs dare not contain.

because a love like ours
was born from stars.

a love like ours
was *meant* to last.

I'm still waiting for that sun
that kissed me farewell
with a promise to return.

I didn't realize sunsets were like that.

I guess I never really knew you.

I would bury myself
within this pain,
over never having felt your sway.

I would press myself
against these thorns,
over never having felt your warmth.

I would burrow
in the melancholy of this wrath,
over never having felt your seraph.

because there are some things that are worth it all.

there are some things that are worth the fall.

I search for
your eyes
in these
grey skies.

the skyline so dull,
yet my dreams
are still alive.

I am not sure
why these clouds
remind me of you.

perhaps it's all hope,
just boundless leaps of faith,

that silver linings
trace your eyes
and the clouds will

send you my way.

sometimes I walk
those paths,
the ones that led us
to the stars.

I sit in absence of your touch,
but I can still feel

your *wonderlust*.

and now
dusk has become
even more melancholic
than the loneliest of nights.

yet I would rather be
wrapped in the claws
of this dark,
than watch beauty unfold

without you

in my arms.

I will dream,
until dying embers
make it impossible
to see, to visualize
you and me.

and then I'll
just cling to hope
that the fire will reignite
and a spark will find us,

in the dead of night.

do you ever look at butterflies
and wonder if, they too,
carry pain?

are there wounds beneath
their silent flight
that they've learnt to disguise?

do their rainbow tipped wings
fold over painful things,

just like a smile?

I don't think I am alone
when I say -
I've held onto love
for too long.

there was always a petal
still attached,

or a leaf
that had not yet, fallen.

I guess that is what makes love so hard.

we see it all

through rose tinted glass.

one moment,
we are caressing the sky.

the next,
we are struggling to fly.

but the hardest part of all,
is not the fall.

it is the digging.

it is the finding
of ourselves again,
in amongst the rubble

of it all.

CHAPTER THREE

All This Hope & Healing

no one told me
how hard those waves
would crash against
my chest.

and not even I knew,
how buoyant
a heart can be
when broken into a
million bits.

perhaps it is true,
even I can find strength,
buried amongst
the debris of my chest.

so, hope, please find me,
together we can
release what love has

enmeshed.

it is amazing how much
the stars and the moon
become our muse
when life paints
us in gloomy hues.

I guess we are all
just trying to find
a way out of the dark.

and the night sky seems like

a good place to start.

even the moon
can become eclipsed
at times.

she is not always whole.
she is sometimes
hard to find.

but she will never
let go of
her entire light.

instead,
she holds on tight,
keeping her
nocturnal mode alive.

for this is how she
survives those darkest nights.

and perhaps, this is how I can retain my own light.

like a burnt forest
covered in ash,
sometimes I too
must mask behind
my remains.

because, often,
the healing is in the hiding.

and then everything starts
to grow back.

everything rises from the ash.

sometimes,

there is such turmoil
folded beneath our skin,
and yet, we still find our smile,
because surface creases
don't ache like the ones within.

and I cannot help but wonder,
if we shared more of what we hide,

would our smiles multiply?

would our folds subside?

I am not sure what
makes me write more.

pain or love?
dark or light?

what I do know is,
the words paint
a picture of my heart,

and sometimes,
it is the simplest words
that bring
color to my dark.

like painting strokes of hope over all of that pain.

can breaths be just like those
winds of time?

is there a way to heal from this
chapter of mine?

perhaps painful exhales
can caress those lines

sweeping words away as
though they no longer hold
weight

maybe breaths can mimic
the dawn of day

I'm hoping all this air draws
sunshine

to every page.

I paint my wings crimson
when it storms like this,
for I must not
lose hope of ever
flying again.

I may flounder
against this rain,
but I shall
fold myself within these wings
and listen to the hum
this autumn shade brings.

remember, new beginnings start with things that fall.

my faith is shaking,

but I still want to believe,
when something breaks,
something stronger is being made.

and I hope, *that something is me.*

hope has hands
that take hold of my dark,
coating me in embers
that bring warmth to my heart.

guides me to those gates
that close behind storms,
and whispers my name

forevermore.

I take my steps
under the moon's eye,
for she's the one I trust
more than I.

she will guide me
when I steer into the night,
she will make
the dark path come to light.

I will not chase her every lit way,
for I will know
what her light has to say.

I know her light is my night's

whisper.

my heart is like a rose
without the thorns.
its stems
tend to weaken
in storms.

its petals fall
when it is shaken,
but it stays alive
with all the noise
it keeps making.

for it seems this rose
always blooms best,
when there is loud
music in my chest.

because a heart that beats strong

can sound just like spring has sprung.

my petals have now
hit the ground,

but I'll keep them
from scattering
too far from my crown.

there is hope
in these blooms,
whether perched up
or down.

now, this garland will stay
in the palm of my hand,

and I'll carry my crown

in a different way.

I'm willing growth
back into these empty spaces
because, if there is one thing
I know for sure,

there is room in here
for so much more

of me.

battle scars
are like sunbeams –

they may not be visible
to the naked eye,
but they are there
reminding you
that you're still alive.

you survived, yet another day.

these tears, I bottle,
and they become
the petrichor that
keeps my feet on
the ground.

reminding me
not all that's grey is wistful

not all that falls dies.

I am still wrapped
in this cocoon.

some days, I wake,
and the layers ache,
they're that tight.

other days, I feel they
have loosened in
the night.

yet, I never stop
reminding myself what is
happening inside.

this butterfly in me

will soon reach the sky.

these shadows
speak to me.

they still move,
despite their dark,
and eventually
find their light
when they fade away.

they whisper

telling me, that I too
can move from
these dark contours,

away from a path
not destined to be,

and find my light, where it is waiting for me.

sometimes hope
looks more like gloom,
but there's always
something
to hold onto.

remind yourself
when you feel all alone,
flowers still bloom
when they are
on their own,

and so can you.

it takes time to peel away the layers
we've grown so accustomed to.

but I assure you,

the unveiling will be a beautiful thing.

butterflies prove
that even delicate things
can find their wings

and so can you.

hope is, waiting
for a sunrise,
knowing
the light
is hard to see at first,

but if you're patient,
you will witness
something
spectacular.

and life is always more beautiful

when the sun comes out.

a heart can stay
hard forever.

or just like rain clouds,

it can learn to let go

and soften again.

I am realizing
that not all that grows
needs light.

you see, some flowers still
bloom at night,

and I know of one
that best defies all odds.

the evening primrose
still blossoms
from her dark pod.

and so can I.

they say we always
land on our feet,
and yet I have lost count
of the number of times
my knees have been
my savior,

anchored me to
the ground when
my feet wished only to
sink in deeper,

and saved my face from
planting the soil
when all I wanted
was to taste my own
ruins.

these feet may keep me walking

but it is these knees that keep me from sinking.

sometimes, flowers
grow in the most
unexpected places,

like blooms
sprouting to life
in between the cracks of
stoned earth.

it makes me wonder if these little miracles are
life's way of reminding us that even the
smallest of things can signify *great* hope.

the ground is
the place I fall onto
when everything
else fails.

for it is down here
that I smell home,
while up there
turns stale.

my roots are bred
in the bone,
and all my seeds here
lay delicately sewn,

just longing to grow

from the essence of home.

cold cannot make a season of me.
it will remain something climatic,
something external.

just like a winter's day
that can chill my hands,

but not my heart.

I have learnt that healing
is sweeter than sour,

and the road to recovery
is often flooded with salted showers.

yet, the tears flow for a higher purpose.

you see, sprinkling salt over fruits
does not make their sweetness dilute.

in-fact, it makes them even sweeter.

a teaspoon of sugar
complements so many things.

and healing is one of them.

not all clouds bring rain.

and perhaps my own clouds
are in vain
because the tears do not flow
like they used to.

and the sky has never looked so beautiful.

I've spent
what seems
like a lifetime
waiting for
sunsets to return.

but now it's time
to let go of what was never mine.

and these sunrises come so effortlessly,
as though they are addressed to me.

just like a new day.

just like a new beginning.

the sun seeps through
the rain,
and then all the magic
rises from
the mundane.

that bridge of soft hues
comes to life
and paints the sky
right before your
very eyes.

one moment dreary,
a wistful grey.
the next, a spectral prism
on display.

if only we could
see life
in the same kind
of way,

always finding
a brighter path,
that bridge of hope,
something that
takes us
to our very own

kaleidoscope.

sometimes, we forget
great things
can grow from tiny seeds.

a forest was not always a forest.

it too was infant.
it too was vulnerable.

I find light in the dark
when I see nothing
beyond.

it has a nocturnal switch
that casts a faint
flicker at my feet,

and shows me,
with such wonder,
how to keep placing
one foot in front
of the other.

because that is what
I need at times,
when somber
casts shadows over
this journey of mine.

and this light I call hope,
is always guiding
my way.
it finds me
on my darkest days

and whispers my name.

I am not sure what I fear more,

dreams that slip through
moonlit fingers
and crash at the floor,

or dreams that land in
the palm of hands
yet slip away
because they were never
meant to stay.

but one thing I will never let fear destroy,

is my will to dream.

I find strength
in my waking hours.

heavy eyes remind me
that I conquered the night.

grey shows me that I am now
a shade away from the dark
and one closer to the light.

it's the little things
that give me strength,

but the strength is *big*.

those clouds fill the day,
but that can only mean one thing –

rain is on its way.

and there can never be
too much water,

for this pain needs
to flow somewhere.

left inside,
tears become nothing more
than a babbling brook
with nowhere to go.

and that's not how I face my pain.

that's not how my healing is gained.

some days, I am more
wild than caught.
other days, I am nothing more
than a caged bird.

but I always find the key
to set me free,
and I always know
the way back in,
if need be.

because some days are for *flying*,

and some days are for *hiding*.

clouds do not have to be dreary things,
in fact, they can spark our dreams.

because watching things change
before our eyes,
can be like envisaging ourselves
evolve and come to life.

there is so much hope in a day
that embraces change,
and we have the power to shape our days

in so many hopeful ways.

love comes so naturally
to the heart,
and yet,
we forget to love ourselves.

perhaps loving others
is fulfillment enough
and we don't feel the need for more.

but when love dies,
we are all we have,

and that's when self-love
becomes
the arms that comfort us.

that's when self-love
becomes

our wings.

sometimes
it is easy to think
that to weep
is to weaken,

but rivers flow inside
that hold the weight
of all that pain.

our hearts carry it all
before we relinquish
to that sea.

and if you ask me,
that is more like strength
than weakness.

fragile is she
too scared to climb
too scared to graze her knees.

but strong is she
who faces the fall
who wipes her knees

and embraces it all.

sadness creeps into our hearts
painting all the beautiful things dark.

but just like heavy clouds
void the blue sky,
as soon as we cry
all that weight subsides.

you see, the art of letting go
paints over dark sorrow.

and the sky returns to a crystal blue,

life becomes more beautiful.

my tears had become
an unfamiliar devour.

every drop turned
from sweet to sour.

it seemed the more I cried
in the witching hour,
the more bitter everything became.

so now, my tears flow more like
a beautiful spring shower,

and I am watching all my fruits,

come back into flower.

cast me away
as a dusty shadow,
yet hope extends
beyond this
forsaken fallow.

I will climb,
I will graze my knees
against the grind,
just searching for the exit route.

whatever it takes,
I will fight it through.

until I meet hope face on.

and this dust adheres to
a shimmery coat,
and I wrap myself in its

layers of hope.

we determine what we dim
and what we light up.

we determine how bright
our own constellation shines.

we know that stars cannot
just be plucked from the sky.

yet we can choose the light
we wish to be surrounded by.

we choose how bright

we want our lives to be.

strength is
not about stepping over
the potholes
and building bridges
over cracked earth.

strength is immersing
ourselves in
all the things that we fear.
facing the dips
and falling within,
letting the earth seep in.

because conditioning our
soil to all that we fear,
is like sowing new seeds

for courage to appear.

somewhere between
sunrise and moonlight,
I must retrieve my grace from
that hiding place.

dress myself
in its layers of forgiveness
and walk away
in an effortless way.

because letting go of weight

makes our journey that much easier.

if there is a mountain to climb,
then I choose a sunny day
because the beauty of warmth
is that it makes everything feel

so much closer.

I hold my moon
to my chest,
for this is the way
my heart beats best.

my lungs may collapse
with the weight of it all,
but she makes them rise
and she makes them fall.

the inhales do not
count so much anymore.
she is the one that drives it all.

she makes it become

one big exhale.

I can comfortably carry
forgiveness in my heart,
for it is light, like a feather
that completes my flight.

opening up the sky for me.

so I can fly.

so I can leave my pain behind.

there are eyes
at the top of the
mountain
looking down at me
with such
shimmering hope.

how powerful
perception can be
when we can see beyond
what is right before us

and rise above
the tribulations
this ground
often weaves us in.

I'll always have faith in my higher self.

I'll always have faith in my mountain's view.

healing starts today.
my feet have finally
hit the ground.

they now stand on their own
and these knees no longer
anchor my fall.

there's a blank canvas
on the wall,
waiting for an impression
such as this.

I need to close
that winter palette.
fold away all the grey,
and paint myself like
a rainbow

paints the day.

healing speaks
in so many ways.

sometimes, it can be
as simple as
opening the curtains
to the day.

sometimes, it is big,
like learning to
peel back things
that sting.

but we cannot rush
a process that tore
our hearts apart,

because putting delicate
things back together
is a fine art,

and one that cannot be learnt easily

in the dark.

these wings may look cute,
but let me tell you -
they don't always fly.
sometimes even
the prettiest parachutes
fall from the sky.

but the butterfly in me,
she never hides for too long.

for there's so much to be seen.
a whole world is

waiting for me.

the breaths of these stars
seem to be in sync
with my own.

I cannot help but wonder
if the night sky
is finally sending me the exhales
I never had the strength

to make on my own.

it's hard to not look up
to big mountains
because that's where
life seems to always be
calling from.

I've reached various peaks
and breathed in the most
spectacular views,

but in all honesty,
there is nothing quite like
the realization that

there is no mountain great enough
or view spectacular enough
to compare with
what's at your very own feet.

contentment is such a beautiful place to reach.

the future looks a lot like spring,
and that's the beauty of healing.
you begin to see things grow.

you begin to see things clearly.

are you noticing, with every day
the pain is fading away?

now, when it rains,
you're not the first to cry.

now, when the sky is grey,
you're not the first to dull.

every day is getting closer

to a brighter you.

I am holding happiness
like it never left,
as though it had remained
folded beneath my skin.
bound to my every heartbeat.
strung to my every breath.

just waiting for me
to let the light back in.

just waiting for me

to start again.

sunrise brings me to my knees.

not with despair,
but with sheer
gratitude and prayer.

that a new day has arrived,
a special gift addressed to me

and I can choose how I live,
I can choose how I wish to be.

I own this day,
it's marked with my name and date

and with every moment,
I shall not hesitate

for there is never any guarantee
of another gift like this,

in-fact, there is never any guarantee

of anything.

with every inhale,
I am letting in peace,
guiding it to my chest
so that my racing heart can rest.

with every exhale,
I am releasing the pain.
I am opening the cavities
where dismay lay.

with every rise and fall,
I am reminding myself,
in some way,
that I have the power
to keep and cast away.

that I hold the key
to all my temple's needs.

that I hold the key to my everything.

I look into mirrors,
and I no longer
hide from what I see.

I will not let
glances of
who I am, bother me.

for this body
is my temple,
my one and
only vessel.

so, I shall look past
these scars
and see them as medallions
for my heart.

and these lines that
I have gained
will not be painted
over in vain.

instead, I will embrace
each crease
and showcase that I
survived
all of this.

I shall focus on the
folds around my eyes,
for therein in lies
the proof that I've smiled

155

a trillion times.

I will look at myself and realize more and more,

I am a warrior.

with a gentle core.

FEATURE WRITER

Marie Tender

Instagram handle @thetenderest

hummingbird wings
fly me through the dewdrops
bathe me in new dreams
let go of falling leaves
cascading to the ground
beneath me

it's a new dawn
and day breaks with
hummingbird wings
feathers against the sunrise –

let it rain.

TERAZA FAULKNER

ABOUT THE AUTHOR

Teraza Faulkner, resides in Perth, Western Australia.

Teraza's poetry was born from a desire
to explore her creative mind.
Her love for nature and the wonder of the night
sky has largely inspired her writing.
Teraza delves into human emotions surrounding
love, hope, loss and healing
in a unique and powerful way.
Every piece is thought provoking and
delivers a powerful message her audience
can connect with.

She is the co-author of an anthology
'Amour Sans Fin'.

Follow Teraza's Instagram page @mymoonandeye.

Lightning Source UK Ltd.
Milton Keynes UK
UKHW041118211221
396027UK00003B/368